Get Motoring!
Motorcycles

by Dalton Rains

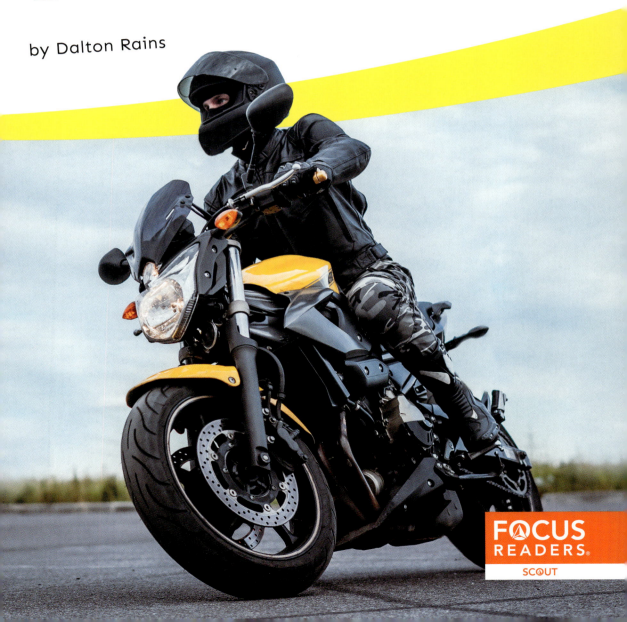

FOCUS READERS. SCOUT

www.focusreaders.com

Copyright © 2024 by Focus Readers®, Mendota Heights, MN 55120. All rights reserved. No part of this book may be reproduced or utilized in any form or by any means without written permission from the publisher.

Focus Readers is distributed by North Star Editions:
sales@northstareditions.com | 888-417-0195

Produced for Focus Readers by Red Line Editorial.

Photographs ©: Shutterstock Images, cover, 1, 4, 7, 9, 11, 13, 15, 16 (top left), 16 (top right), 16 (bottom left), 16 (bottom right)

Library of Congress Cataloging-in-Publication Data
Names: Rains, Dalton, author.
Title: Motorcycles / by Dalton Rains.
Description: Mendota Heights, MN : Focus Readers, [2024] | Series: Get motoring! | Includes index. | Audience: Grades K-1
Identifiers: LCCN 2023029829 (print) | LCCN 2023029830 (ebook) | ISBN 9798889980094 (hardcover) | ISBN 9798889980520 (paperback) | ISBN 9798889981374 (pdf) | ISBN 9798889980957 (ebook)
Subjects: LCSH: Motorcycles--Juvenile literature.
Classification: LCC TL440.15 .R35 2024 (print) | LCC TL440.15 (ebook) | DDC 629.227/5--dc23/eng/20230627
LC record available at https://lccn.loc.gov/2023029829
LC ebook record available at https://lccn.loc.gov/2023029830

Printed in the United States of America
Mankato, MN
012024

About the Author

Dalton Rains is a writer and editor who lives in Minnesota.

Table of Contents

Motorcycles 5

Parts 8

Uses 12

Glossary 16

Index 16

road →

Motorcycles

Motorcycles drive on roads.

They help people travel.

Riders sit on top of

the motorcycle.

One or two people can ride.

They wear **helmets**.

Helmets help people stay safe.

Parts

A motorcycle has two **wheels**.

It also has **headlights** in front.

A motorcycle has **handlebars**. The rider twists the right handle to go faster. The rider squeezes the brake to slow down.

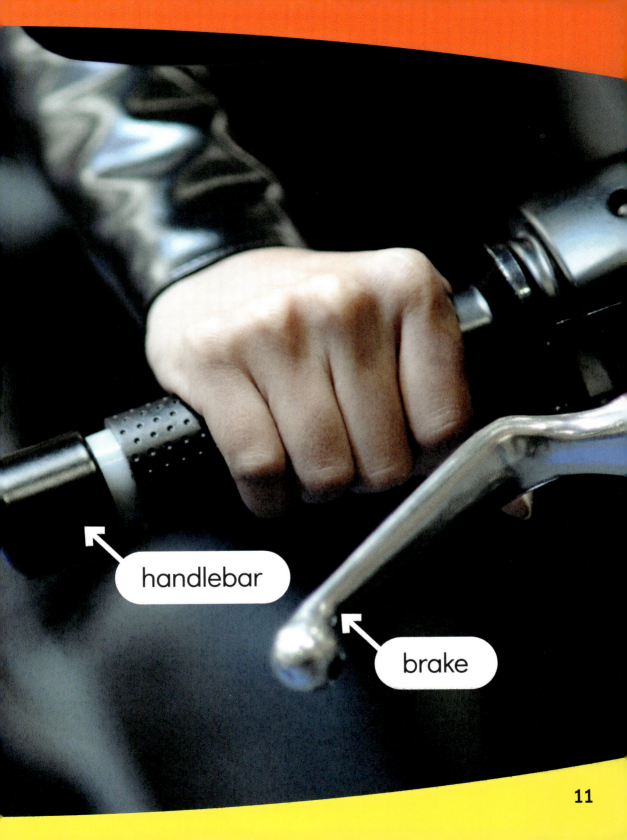

Uses

Some motorcycles go very fast.

They can make quick turns.

Some people use them to race.

Other people like to ride motorcycles for fun.

They ride with friends.

They explore different places.

Glossary

handlebars

helmets

headlights

wheels

Index

B
brake, 10

F
friends, 14

H
handle, 10

R
roads, 5